Tell someone
you love them

FIESTA
of HAPPINESS

Tell someone
you love them

David Baird

MQP

Introduction

What is love anyway?

Love is an exceptional force.

Can we measure it? No.

We can't see it either,

Yet it has the power to transform lives in an instant

And bring more joy to more people than

Any other thing.

It is freely available to all,

Rich and poor

Regardless of age, race, gender, or physical ability,

It can be given by anyone

To anyone and is even better to receive!
Far too much of it is wasted on things,
Instead of people, and quite often
We miss the chance to express it –
And live to regret it.
Which is why,
If you feel love for someone in your heart,
You should always,
In the best way you know how,
Tell them.

It must be love

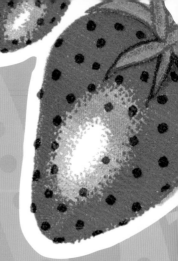

If you suddenly find
You are finishing each other's sentences,
Can't stop gazing into each other's eyes:
That you live for shared moments,
Cuddles and sunsets;
That you go out of your way
To make each other laugh;
That you'd do anything in the world
To make that person happy;
That your heart skips when you see each other
And you close your eyes on the telephone to try to
Get closer to them;
If you feel
You're the only two people in the world,

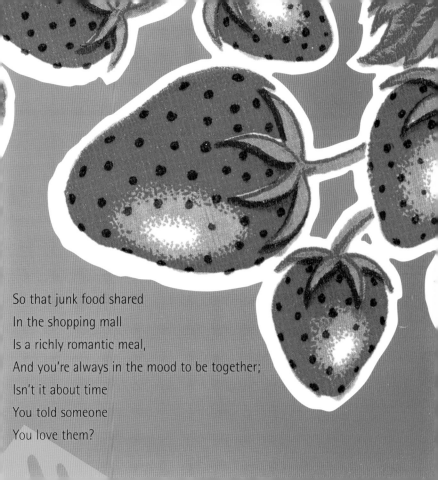

So that junk food shared
In the shopping mall
Is a richly romantic meal,
And you're always in the mood to be together;
Isn't it about time
You told someone
You love them?

Love is something to treasure

There is a timeless excitement about
Embarking on a treasure hunt,
Even if it's only looking for a few hidden eggs
In the garden at Easter
Or a "hot" and "cold" search for an object in a room.
Leave your lover written clues
Along a trail that ends eventually
At a hidden gift that perfectly expresses
Your love for them.

Fall in love with something

There is nothing on this earth
To compare with the feeling and motivation
That flow from being in love.
Some love their car,
Tweenies love pop idols,
Others love their partners,
And some even love their jobs.
Today tune in to the something
That triggers those feelings in you,
And feel the glow
As the happiness of being in love
Floods you from tip to toe.

A bed of roses

Ah, Sunday morning.
No deadlines to beat,
No meetings to attend . . .
While your true love gently sleeps,
Why not silently scatter flowers
And petals all over the bed?
Leave your lover there
To wake at leisure
And work out what has happened,
And what it all means.
Make sure you're not too far away
When realisation dawns!

Get the message?

See if you can outwit each other
By finding new and ever more inventive ways
To communicate your love for each other.
One might write it across the bathroom mirror
With lipstick,
While the other might discover it
Spelled out in jam across a slice of bread.
Other places could include:
A piece of sticky-back plastic stuck
On to a watchface,

On the forehead of your sleeping lover,
Inside a shoe,
On a fresh pat of butter,
Hanging on the washing line . . .
The possibilities are endless,
And it's always heartwarming
To discover a new message
When and where you least expect it.

Sunset serenade

It can be contained no longer!
You're bursting to tell someone you love them.
Well, take the message to the one you love.
Line up a mariachi band
Or musicians from a local Greek restaurant
And stand beneath the window
Of the target of your affection.
Then, as the music gently drifts
Through the scented evening air,
And you catch a glimpse of your heart's desire,
Framed behind curtains,
Throw up a flower
With a note attached that says:
"I love you".

18 tell someone you love them

Make an exhibition of yourselves

Carry a camera, one each,
Around with you for a fortnight
And set about capturing each other
In ways that show the reasons why you love:
Gestures, smiles, thoughtful moments, snoozing,
Sadness, excitement, sulks . . .
Then get the films developed
And in your flat, house, garage, studio
Or wherever else you can find
Two big bare walls,
Hang them and title them.
Each exhibition of photographs
Will help you see yourselves
Through your lover's eyes.

Oh, by the way...

One of the most intriguing ways
Of arousing your partner's attention
Is to wait
Until they are in the midst of a serious conversation,
Then lean over and whisper
"I love you" in their ear
But carry on as if nothing untoward had passed.
They'll be highly unlikely
To get you out of their thoughts
For the rest of the day . . .
And probably the rest of their lives!

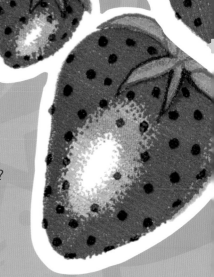

Just say it...

"I love you!"
What's so difficult about saying that?
If you find it hard
Or you need some romantic support,
Put on a recording that
Pulls at the heartstrings
And ask your partner to dance.
Once they are in your embrace, whisper to them to
Close their eyes
And imagine a special place –
Say a beach in Bali at sunset,
A hilltop in Crete on a moonlit night –
And make sure that they see the picture.

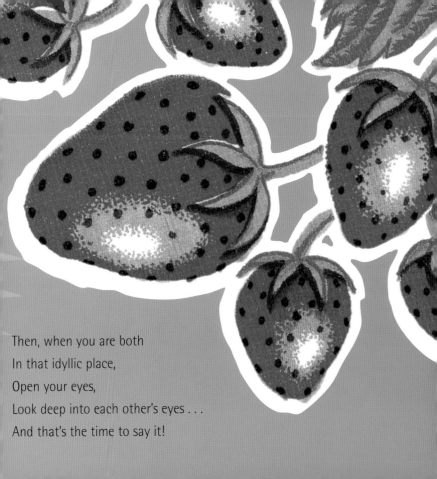

Then, when you are both
In that idyllic place,
Open your eyes,
Look deep into each other's eyes . . .
And that's the time to say it!

The a-z of love

There doesn't have to be a birthday,
Christmas or other celebration
As a reason for giving gifts.
Cleverly accumulate
An alphabetical cache of presents,
One for every letter: for example,
An arrow (Cupid's, of course!),
A balalaika (to serenade with),
A cassette (of love songs) . . . and so on,
Then wait for a good time,
Like when your partner
Is down in the dumps
Or at the start of a perfect weekend,
And let the gifts cascade
On the one you love.

To the ends of the earth

"I can't imagine a day without you!"
Is the cry of lovers who've grown
So intertwined that they'll never know
Just how it would feel . . .
Unless they give each other the chance!
Pack yourselves off
In separate directions for a couple of days.
One could go to Lands End
While the other heads for John O'Groats.
Know the bittersweet pain
Of communicating feelings to each other
Over a distance,
Then savour the very special bliss
Of being reunited.

Scent by code

At some stage,
Slip into your conversation
That you heard of a couple
Who created a secret code of scents.
With it they could say things like
"I miss you", or "I love you",
Depending on which scent they used.
Suggest that you play a similar game,
And devise your own code.

Rose could mean "I love you"
Lavender could represent longing,
Camomile could tell your loved one
You're sad . . . and so on.
Sensitise your noses
By trying a few aromatherapy oils,
Then set the ball rolling
By sending a letter to your lover at work
That clearly conveys how much you love them!

Painted love

Before you next invite
Your true love round for dinner,
Commission an artist to paint their portrait
From your favourite photograph.
Have it framed
Then mount it on a wall
Where it can be easily seen.
Tuck a small envelope marked for your lover
Into the frame and watch as they open it
To find a card inside that simply says:
"I love this picture."

Go awol with love

These days
Our work seems the master of all that we do,
The pigeonhole for who we are,
And often it is this
That drives a wedge into relationships.
Well wise up!
Your relationship means everything
And if it looks to be on the rocks,
Or heading in that perilous direction,
Perhaps you'd better play truant for the day
And spend it together.
Enjoy each other's company,
Selfishly make plans together
And have fun carrying them out.
Go out on an afternoon date for a change, then
End your day with a late-night walk
Holding hands.

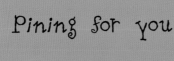

Pining for you

I once knew someone
  Who had to work away from home
    At a sensitive time in his relationship.
      He would immerse himself in his work
        And she would get lost in her gardening.
        One day the doorbell rang at home.
          When she went to answer it
      She was flummoxed to find the local nurseryman
    Bearing a large potted conifer
      When she read the card
      To see who it was from,
      The message she read was:
      "Pining for you!"

Shout it out

Make it public.

We all want to!

The moment we feel sure and good and secure

In our relationship

We don't mind the whole world knowing about it.

We walk hand in hand

Or embrace passionately,

We neck and canoodle and rarely try to hide it.

The next time there's a village fete

Or a charity bazaar,
Why not get the message out strong and clear
Over the public-address system?
You can hear it now . . .
"Anyone who has lost a shoe
Can find it in the organiser's tent.
And the dark-haired chap from the garage
Wants the red-haired lady from the vet's
To know that he's in love with her!"

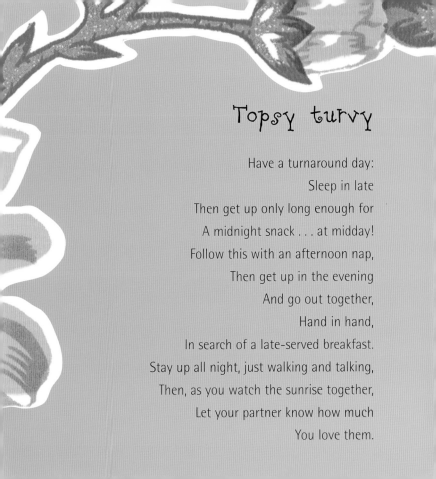

Topsy turvy

Have a turnaround day:
Sleep in late
Then get up only long enough for
A midnight snack . . . at midday!
Follow this with an afternoon nap,
Then get up in the evening
And go out together,
Hand in hand,
In search of a late-served breakfast.
Stay up all night, just walking and talking,
Then, as you watch the sunrise together,
Let your partner know how much
You love them.

Get down and flirty

After a while, in every relationship,
Things begin to be taken for granted.
We are always together,
Always at hand.
There's little variation from the routine
And things can become . . . well . . .
Stale.
But remember what it was like
To flirt with your lover?
How it was when you were

Getting to know each other?
Why not pick a perfect moment
And get that fire going again?
Dedicate a day
To flirting with your partner,
And by the time the moon comes up
You'll both be primed
To say and show how much
You love each other.

Special delivery

Find out a time when
The love of your life is going to be at home
And arrange for something special
To be delivered to them there.
It could be a spectacular gift
Or just a simple envelope,
Containing nothing more
Than a small piece of paper with
"I love you" written on it.

Song sung true

Sometimes we have to do that little bit extra
For someone to sit up and notice us.
At times like this
It helps to enlist the services of
A singing telegram!
For a nominal amount of money
These brave souls will go to
Your loved one's place of work,
Or their home,
And deliver, in song, your heartfelt sentiments.

If you really want to do
The whole Hollywood thing,
You could make an appearance halfway through
And slowly approach with a bunch of flowers
Or a bottle of champagne.
By the time you reach the end of that long walk
You will know whether
Telling this particular someone
That you love them
Was a good idea.

Love hearts

These pretty little sweets exist
In some form or other all over the world,
So if you can't find them
Ask a friend to search for some for you.
Each pastel disc is embossed with
A loving phrase, such as, "Be mine",
"True heart", "Fax me" and more.
Present your lover with a love heart
At frequent intervals throughout the day
And, last thing at night,
Leave one on the pillow that says
"I love you".
What a perfect day.

La bella luna

Choose a beautiful moonlit night.
Grab your partner by the hand
And run off to somewhere silent
With lots of space and privacy
Where you can clearly see the stars.
Lie together on the ground
Looking up at that glowing orb.
Tell your lover to stare at it closely
And to listen very hard . . .
Then, as they do so,
Turn your lips to their ear and whisper:
"I love you" on a soft warm breath.

Special place

Take a day off
And with the love of your life,
Go out together to search for, and discover,
A place that you can call
Your "Special Place" . . .
A place that can be easily reached,
Where you can both go
Whenever the mood comes upon you,
Or visit alone
During times apart, to feel closer to each other.
Find that place
And secure it in your hearts
By telling each other there
That you love them.
It will remain your Special Place
For all time.

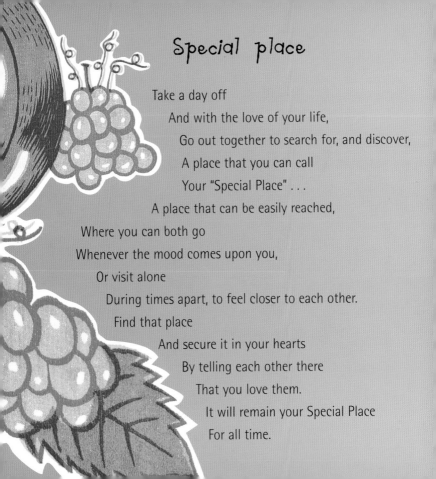

Well versed

Roses are red,
Violets are blue,
La la la . . . hmm hmm . . . doo doo!
It doesn't have to rhyme to be a love poem.
Just know what it is that you really want to say
And be as full, as truthful,
As descriptive as you can.
Then stand back
And watch it melt the heart of the one it was
Intended for.

Sunny delight

Keeping love bottled up inside
Is like never allowing the sun to shine.
Get into the habit of daily telling someone
That you love them,
Whether it's your partner
Or your maiden aunt twice removed
Who lives on the other side of the world,
Your friend, your family, your cleaner,

Whoever . . .
With your voice,
Either in person or by telephone,
By postcard, letter, poem
Or even by carrier-pigeon if you have to.
Get those three little words out
And don't let yourself go to bed at night
Without having done so.
Let the sun shine!

Love letters

Take a hint from the French novelist
Gustave Flaubert when it comes to love letters . . .
Who could resist your charms
If you were to write and declare
That you'll cover them with your love
When next you see them,
With caresses, with ecstasy.
That you want to feast them
With all the joys of the flesh,
So that they faint and feel that they've gone to heaven.

That you want them to be astonished by you,
And to confess to themselves
That they'd never even dreamed
Of such transports . . .
That you want them, when they are old,
To recall those heartstopping hours,
That you want their dry bones to quiver with joy
Whenever they think of you . . .
Why put it off?
Put pen to paper and compose your prose.

Read all about it

The news can be depressing at the best of times,
But if your lover is a commuter
You could brighten up their day
In this headline-grabbing way.
Seize the newspaper as soon as it comes
And secretly go through it,
Writing loving things within the body of the text
Wherever there are gaps.
Hand it over at the moment of parting
So they only discover your handiwork
During their journey on the 8.22.

Message in a bottle

Slip a love letter
Into someone's briefcase
Or lunchbox,
Slide one into their sports kit
Or hide one in a handkerchief,
Stick one to the sunvisor of their car
Tie one to the tip of their umbrella
Or wedge one into their wallet.
And you needn't be stranded on a desert island
To pop one into a bottle:
Put one out with the empties on the doorstep
To make your milkman's day.

Hand in hand

When was the last time
You held hands in public?
Remember back to the time
When you did so often,
Without giving it a second thought,
And how exceptional
The feeling of togetherness was.
See if you can rekindle now.
The next time you're in a public place
Take that hand lovingly in yours.
That says it all.
If it's your very first go,
Don't think about it –
Just do it
And in no time at all you'll soon
Be dab hands.

A giant step

Make your own lunar landing.

Plant your flag for the universe to see

And on it proclaim your love.

Of course, getting to the real moon may present problems.

But how about a lunar cake?

Decorate a cake to resemble the moon,

Find a model astronaut in a toy shop

And write "I love you" on a little flag.

Set the items in the icing
Then present it to your true love atmospherically,
With lights dimmed,
Music playing
And a candle or two.
One small step for a cake,
One giant leap for a couple!

We like to hear it

You can't hurt anyone
By telling them you love them.
They may even surprise you
And love you back.
Everyone would prefer to be loved
Than be unloved!
And no matter how much
"In love" we feel,
We still like to be regularly told
That we're loved,
Because those three little words
Add up to so much.
So say them often:
"I love you."

Advertising your emotions

One sure method
Of getting the message across
Is to hire the billboard
Opposite your loved one's place of work.
Have "I LOVE YOU" in capital letters
Ten feet tall
Blazoned for all the world to see –
And, if you're feeling very brave,
You could include your photograph.

Webbed feat

Those of us with a penchant for computing
Could create a website devoted to our love,
With animated gifs, jpegs, little films,
Lines from Shakespeare's sonnets,
Poems of our own,
And photographs,
And call it something obvious, like

www.iloveyoususiewoo.com.
Alternatively, the more private couple,
Who like their online space to be secret,
Could create a web address
Of numbers and letters that only they
Will know how to access . . .
And no one else ever know of!

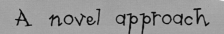

A novel approach

Take a block of time,
A bigger block of paper
And a nice sharp pencil,
Then write about you and your lover
As if you were the central characters
Of a steamy romantic novel.
Hold nothing back on the page,
Let the kisses linger
And put all you feel
Into your character's declaration of undying love.
Then leave your unpublished manuscript
Lying somewhere to be discovered and read
By your partner.

Foreign affairs

We can't always do the Hollywood thing
Of romantically sending word of our affection,
Scratched out by candlelight, under canvas on
Safari in Africa, to our sweetheart back home . . .
But here's the next best thing!
Many bric-a-brac shops and antiques fairs
Have stocks of old and exotic postcards,
Among which some are still unused.
Buy a supply to send to your lover,
For, even though you may be writing it in the office
Next to the intended recipient, the illusion remains
Strong and the essence of romance and

Hint of the exotic make for a potent mixture.

For instance,

If you can find a postcard from India,

Perhaps with an elephant on it

Or the Taj Mahal, write to your loved one

As though you were there,

Longing for them to be with you;

Describe the long nights, the sounds, the smells,

Your excitement at the prospect of being reunited –

And, of course,

Be certain to proclaim your undying love.

Aerial display

You've sent the flowers
And bought the chocolates,
Done the romantic walks on the beach,
And now you want to really make your mark
In the affections of your loved one.
How about hiring a sky-writing pilot to
Trace those three little words high up with the clouds
Where they cannot be missed?
Or book a lesson in a biplane
For your sweetheart, so that when they're airborne
They'll look down and see the giant "I LOVE YOU"
You've marked out in a field
Using white ribbon!

Riddle of the sands

Take your mate to the seaside
To a secluded beach.
Ask them to sit and wait ten minutes before
Following in the direction you take.
Sort of a Hide and Seek game.
Then set off and when you are just out of sight
Write your true feelings about that person
In the sand.
Watch their reaction
To the words.
The look on their face as they join you
Will reveal to you whether those feelings
Are mutual.

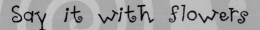

Say it with flowers

There are different flowers for different months,
For different birthdates and different occasions.
There are so many varieties available
That we can say almost anything with flowers.
But you still can't beat
A beautiful long-stemmed single red rose
Presented with a long and lingering kiss.
If you want to add a finishing touch,
Whisper
"I love you"
As your partner inhales its scent.

In my gondola

A memorable way of saying
"I love you"
Is to tell your partner
To wait outside their place of work
One Friday night
And have their passport with them!
Whisk them off to the airport,
Check yourselves in
And fly off to somewhere romantic
For the weekend.

If it is Venice, hire a gondola
With a singing gondolier,
Pour some champagne
And tell your sweetheart
There and then that
You love them.
Wherever you take them,
By the time that you arrive back home
You'll have created a lasting memory
And made a loving relationship
Still more of a certainty.

It takes two to tango

The most romantic and
Without doubt the sexiest dance of all time
Is the tango.
Keep your eyes open for public workshops
For this passion rouser
And enrol yourself and your true love.
Don't tell them where you are taking them –
Just suggest what clothes they should wear.
They're bound to be amazed.
In the final moments of the course,
When you're dancing together like pros,
Annouce with Latin passion:
"I love you".

Love bites

A food lover's way to spread some cheer
And make your feelings very clear
Is to cut some sandwiches into letters
And take your beau off on a picnic.
Find a lovely secluded, romantic spot,
By a river, in a wood or amid a meadow,
Then, as you set out the feast,
Arrange the food into the words
"I love you" on the plate.
If the feeling proves to be mutual,
You'll be made to eat your words!

The best-laid plans

There is no single formula
To tell someone you love them
That works for everyone.
Look carefully at the person you love
And think about all the things they enjoy
The little things that make them happy.
Above all, make sure that you enjoy the time you spend
Together and that you know enough about each
Other to spring your declaration with out ruining things
It might seem utterly romantic to you
To picnic on a deserted beach at sunset,
Toss a pair of lobsters into the flames
Open a bottle and say, "I love you."
But if you haven't paid attention
You may well discover too late
That your true love hates shellfish
And that smoke gets in their eyes . . .

Dinner for two

Arrange to have a dinner for two
In a unique setting.
Lay out all the trimmings –
Silver cutlery, candles, wine bucket, etc. –
And have somebody serve you
(Dressed for the part, of course).
Where could this romantic dining date unfold?
How about in a gardener's shed on an allotment,
In a treehouse, or a field on a warm summer evening?
Perhaps aboard a boat,
Or the carriage of an old steam train:
Whatever fires your imagination.
Whatever would be the ideal setting
To tell someone you love them.

Love thru a lens

Imagine your eyes are the camera
And your heart is the album.
Take a good long look,
And see if there is one essential thing
That you can photograph
That will remind you of your lover
And remain with you for the rest of your life.
Take a mental picture,
And whenever you close your eyes
You will always be able to recapture
That moment, that place,
That feeling, that face.

You're gorgeous

We all of us know we have
Certain things about us
That we don't find pleasant,
And we try to deal with them.
None of us wants the person who's supposed to be
The love of our life constantly expounding to us
Just how gruesome we are.
What we do need
For a relationship to flourish and grow
Is some encouragement . . . an occasional reference

To what it is about us

That is lovable!

These little boosts

Can help us to drag up our self-esteem

By the seat of the pants

And make us more secure in ourselves.

If you really want to fill your relationship with roses

Don't prick your lover with their own thorns . . .

Tell them something nice about themselves.

Start with a smile

If you're not quite ready to tell someone
You love them
Then why not start with a loving smile!
Loving smiles cost nothing.
They're always available
And are the most wonderful gift
To give to others.
If you don't believe me,
Look in the mirror
When you're feeling down
Then look at yourself with a loving smile
And you'll see which face makes you feel better.

The best place for sharing such smiles
Is out in the street,
Even among strangers.
Pass a loving smile to a passer-by
And watch as it spreads
From person to person.

True believer

If you can wake up
Facing the truth about your love,
Truth will be your companion
All through your day
And your love will remain true love.
The people you love whom you meet today
Are hungering and thirsting for truth.
Give them the truth about your love,
And they will love you for being truthful.

Initial attraction

Was there ever a more definite
Or longlasting way of saying "I love you"
Than taking a pocketknife,
Climbing a tree, and carving your and your true love's
Initials inside a heartshape on the tree bark?
Damaging trees is frowned on these days,
But there are still many places to
Formalise your feelings, such as gateposts, sheds
And banisters, desks, chairs,
Doors or even . . . if you're absolutely certain that
What you feel will last . . .
On a panel of your car!

Call off the search

Be careful now!
Don't miss a chance to stand still
And let love appear before you.
It's always closer than you think!
When it does reveal itself,
Don't be afraid to say what you feel;
Never be frightened
To tell someone you love them.
If you are, and you don't,
You might become stuck
On the precarious path that winds in and out
Of all the places
Where people suspect that love can be found . . .
But rarely is.

Learn to say i love you

"Ich liebe dich."
 Become a multilinguist:
 There's not a country in the world
 That doesn't have in its language,
A way of saying "I love you".
 If you learnt only this simple phrase,
        You could go anywhere in the world and
          Get closer to the people you meet.
            Learn to say "I love you"
              In several languages, then try out the phrase on
              People you meet who speak those languages.
              Just smile,
            And with a serious and curious look on your face
          Bravely blurt it out.
        Some may slink away thinking you're mad,
          But the chances are that mostly
            They will mirror your warmth.

How to say "I love you" in lots of languages:

Afrikaans	Ek is lief vir jou
Bengali	Aami tomaake bhaalo baashi
Burmese	Chit pa te
Cheyenne	Ne mohotatse
Chinese	Ngo oi ney (Cantonese)
Croatian	Volim te
Czech	Miluji te
Danish	Jeg elsker dig
Greek	S'ayapo (pronounced s'agapo)
Hawaiian	Aloha wau ia oi

Hungarian	Szeretlek
Lebanese	Bahibak
Russian	Ya tyebya lyublyu
Swahili	Nakupenda
Swedish	Jag a'lskar dig
Thai	Chan raak ther
Tunisian	Ha eh bak
Turkish	Seni seviyorum
Welsh	Rwy'n dy garu di
Yiddish	Ikh hob dikh lib

Where there's a will...

Why do we hesitate
Angst-ridden,
Too afraid to proclaim our love?
If we miss the chance,
We'll regret it for the rest of our lives.
So, don't just sit there . . .
Climb up on the roof and shout it out,
Tie a balloon to every tree,
Put an ad in the local paper,

Advertise it on the side of a bus,
Commission a radio jingle,
Knit it into a giant jumper,
Hold up a banner at a football match,
Hire cheerleaders to chant it out,
Anything . . .
But don't just sit there!
If you want someone to know you love them,
You'll have to find a way to tell them.

Chemical reaction

Are you aware
That chocolate shares a chemical with us
That is found in the human brain?
It is called phenylethylamine
And is directly related to the emotional highs
And lows of being in love!
It's a completely natural substance.
So if you're seeking the rush of love . . .
Be sure to give your intended
A big assortment of the very best chocolates
And with every bite
They'll hear you say:
"I love you!"

Published by MQ Publications Limited
12 The Ivories, 6-8 Northampton Street, London N1 2HY
Tel: 020 7359 2244   Fax: 020 7359 1616
e-mail: mail@mqpublications.com

Design: Balley Design Associates

ISBN: 1-84072-429-3

Printed and bound in China